1 MONTH OF
FREE
READING

at

www.ForgottenBooks.com

By purchasing this book you are eligible for one month membership to ForgottenBooks.com, giving you unlimited access to our entire collection of over 1,000,000 titles via our web site and mobile apps.

To claim your free month visit:

www.forgottenbooks.com/free893034

ISBN 978-0-265-81103-0
PIBN 10893034

THE PINE KNOT

VOLUME I.   1910   PRICE $2.50

PUBLISHED ANNUALLY BY

THE STUDENTS OF ATLANTIC CHRISTIAN COLLEGE

TO

MRS. SALLIE F. DUNLAP

LADY PRINCIPAL OF

ATLANTIC CHRISTIAN COLLEGE

out of regard for her being the students' friend, and for her sweet

Christian character, we dedicate this the first volume of

"THE PINE KNOT"

MRS. SALLIE F. DUNLAP

ೞ

MRS. DUNLAP was educated at Alabama State Normal, Florence, Ala.; taught' in the city schools, Dallas, Texas; Chickasaw Colle-giate Institute, Ardmore, Okla.; Fairmont College, Sulphur, Ky.; became Lady Principal and Instructor in Mathematics at Atlantic Christian College, September, 1909.

Mrs. Dunlap is a woman of refined tastes and deep sympathies. She understands the minds and hearts of young men and young women, and with her love for young people can enter into their sorrows and joys and prove to them that invaluable friend and adviser and guide which they so much need in their school days. She has a keen perceptive power, and a true insight into human nature. In the one short year which she has been at Atlantic Christian College she has proven her great worth as an instructor, friend and adviser, and has thus endeared herself to every one with whom she has come in contact. Her work has been of endless value to every one who has come under her influence, and it is to be hoped that she will ever remain at dear old A. C. C. in order that those who follow in the days to come may enjoy the same joys and blessings which those of 1909-'10 have enjoyed.

ATLANTIC CHRISTIAN COLLEGE·

ღ

IT IS difficult to write the history of· an institution so young as Atlantic
Christian College, or to tell of its true position in the educational world,
for it takes years ever to bring out the real usefulness of a college, and,
just as the seeds must lie in the soil for a season before they germinate, sprout,
and bring forth fruit, so the truths and principles and high ideals implanted
in the minds and hearts· of young men and young women require years, and
often many years, to bring forth the greatest results and to show the true usefulness and worth of the institution. It takes not only years, but generations
to record the true position of an educational institution. It is a long time
between seed-time and harvest.

Considering all of this, Atlantic Christian College has a bright and encouraging history, though short and incomplete. And from the few victories
which are to-day visible, we can look for a history filled to the overflowing
with remarkable victories and achievements, when the decades have added
their mosses to·its walls·and when the seeds have had time to sprout in the
minds of the men and women who have received their inspiration and training under its guidance.

The members of the Christian Church in North Carolina long felt the
need of an institution of higher education within this State where the young
men and young women from the· homes of the members of the Christian
Church, as well as from every home, could have an opportunity of a thorough
college training under Christian influence, and where young men who wished
to prepare themselves for the Christian ministry could receive a thorough and
complete Biblical training without having to leave this State, and thus being
lost to the work of the church in North Carolina. The opportunity for the
realization of this desire came in·the Fall of 1901, when the property of the
Kinsey Seminary, located at Wilson, N. C., was offered to the North Carolina
Christian Missionary. Convention in convention assembled at Kinston. The
property was new and up-to-date in every respect. The building had been
·erected in 1898 for Prof. Joseph Kinsey. Prof. Kinsey used the building—
operating Kinsey Seminary—until 1901, when on account of failing health

COLLEGE BUILDING.

he was compelled to give up school work. Prof. Kinsey, together with the other trustees and owners, very liberally gave over his interest in the building and entered into the work of establishing Atlantic Christian College. A campaign was made for money to furnish the building and to make needed repairs. The people took hold of the idea with enthusiasm and earnestness. Dr. J. C. Coggins, a North Carolinian, at that time minister of the Christian Church at Decatur, Ill., was called to the presidency. He made a thorough canvass of the State, and created quite an interest wherever he went. The college opened September, 1902, with more students than could be accommodated, several had to be refused admission. The trustees began the planning for new buildings. But soon the enthusiasm wore off. There were other disadvantages, and at the close of the second year it seemed that failure was inevitable. A number of mistakes had been made. The people had lost confidence in the school, and it looked like the doors would never be opened again. A new president must be found—a man that could tide over the stormy sea. The trustees began to look around. There was only one man whom they thought could redeem the day. That was a man known all over North Carolina. A man who had served his State in many ways, in the legislative halls, in the schoolroom, and in the pulpit. A man of such straightforward character and loving Christian qualities that everyone knew him only to love and respect him. A call went out to him, and Dr. J. J. Harper became president of Atlantic Christian College at the close of the second year—1904. Dr. Harper was a man of action, and had already planned other work for his latter years. He was preparing to write a *History of the Christian Church in North Carolina,* but he laid everything else aside and threw himself into the work of building up Atlantic Christian College, for the establishment of which he had labored so earnestly, and which he had had the honor to name. He labored against difficulties; he sacrificed every personal interest; his whole thought and ambition was to redeem the college and give to it its rightful position in the educational realm of North Carolina and in the minds and hearts of the people of the State. It was up-hill business, but steadily his earnestness and endeavor brought forth results. The attendance the third year was better than at first was thought it could be. The fourth year it was still better, and the fifth year it was better than ever before, and the buildings were taxed to their utmost capacity.

The college was made stronger than ever before. The people gained confidence in it. Dr. Harper had done a work which no other person could have done. But the call came to him to return to his first work. He was advan-

GIRLS' DORMITORY.   BOYS' DORMITORY IN DISTANCE.

cing in years, and he thought that a younger and more active man could probably do better. He asked the trustees to release him. Upon this request, in the Spring of 1907, Mr. J. C. Caldwell, then minister of the Christian Church at Selma, Ala., but who had had much experience in school work, having been president of a college in Kentucky for three years, a graduate of Kentucky University and Yale University, was asked to visit the school with a view to taking up the presidency when Dr. Harper gave it up. Mr. Caldwell and the trustees thought that it would be better for Dr. Harper to continue as president of the college for at least another year. Mr. Caldwell was called to the pastorate of the Wilson Christian Church and was also made dean of the faculty of the college. With this arrangement—the combination of youth and age, of enthusiasm and conservatism of the two giants, Mr. Caldwell and Dr. Harper—the college moved steadily onward. The sixth year was the best in the history of the college up to that time. The attendance was better than ever before, the faculty was stronger, and the grade of work was of a higher order. It was truly the beginning of a brighter and better day. But just in the middle of the year a great calamity befell the college, and every heart was filled with sorrow and grief, for after a brief illness the beloved president, Dr. Harper, was called up higher to his greater reward. No man probably ever did more for the furtherance of the interest and the ideals of a college than Dr. Harper did for Atlantic Christian College, and no one was probably ever loved more for what he did or for the sweet Christian character which he always manifested. This was an hour of gloom for the college, but Mr. Caldwell was master of the situation. Every student realized that the best way to show his love for Dr. Harper was to remain at his post and do all in his power to build up the college. Not a single one left. Mr. Caldwell was at once elected president. He had been associated very closely with Dr. Harper and knew his plans and his ideals, and throwing into these his own youth and vigor and high ideals carried the work onward and upward towards the greater success.

Mr. Caldwell is an exceptionally strong man; a man who can look into the future and plan, and then has the practical ability to work out his plans. As a preacher he ranks among the best; as a business man he grasps the practical side of life and takes every step for the best advantage, and as a teacher he has few equals. North Carolina is fortunate to have such a man in its midst. Under his management the college has gone forward and will continue to go forward more rapidly as the days go by.

DR. J. J. HARPER.

Already you can find the graduates and former students of Atlantic Christian College filling the important positions in life, and wherever they have gone they have made good. We have yet to find the failure among the Alumni of Atlantic Christian College, and we feel that the search will be long before such a one can be found. Steadily the young men and young women who have gone out from the halls of old Atlantic Christian College have been making their way in life, and within a few years they will stand upon the top of the ladder of success.

To-day, Atlantic Christian College writes her history in silver, but to-morrow she will write it in gold. To-day the seeds are just germinating; to-morrow they will sprout and grow and bring forth the mighty oaks of intellectual strength, and beauty and splendor. To-day her sons and daughters are climbing—some of them just beginning the mighty struggle—but to-morrow they will take their stand among the mighty men and women of the United States, the flower of American civilization—the bone and sinew of American power and wealth—the trained, Christian manhood and woman-hood of this the brightest land in all the universe.

All hail, to thee, dear A. C. C.
.All hail, thou fount of knowledge,
All hail, my Alma Mater, hail,
Thou sunny, Southern college.

DR. J. C. CALDWELL.

JESSE COBB CALDWELL

ʊ

JESSE COBB CALDWELL was born in Clay County, Missouri, in 1873, and has just reached the prime -meridian of life. He came from a family, illustrious as politicians, teachers and preachers, and who ever have been champions of higher education. Tracing their ancestry from the great Protector of English liberty, Oliver Cromwell, the Caldwell family early emigrated to America, settled in Virginia and North Carolina, and their descendants are scattered throughout the Union.

Mr. Caldwell graduated from the High School of Excelsior Springs, Mo., in 1892; he entered Kentucky University and took his A. B. degree in 1896; he then pursued the Biblical and Classical courses in the College of the Bible, at Lexington, Ky., and graduated in 1897. He was immediately called to the pastorate of the Christian Church at Owenton, Ky., where he remained six years.

During the last two years of this pastorate, the teaching instinct, woven in the tissues of the family, asserted itself so strongly that Mr. Caldwell was induced to revivify the dying work in a college at Owenton, and he achieved such a decided success that a strong impetus was given to educational work in that section. So great was this impetus that the city of Owenton purchased the property of Caldwell College at a large increase in price.

It was during this ministry also that Mr. Caldwell married, in 1898, Miss Mary Settle, the eldest daughter of Congressman E. E. Settle, who represented the famous Ashland District of Kentucky in Congress, and was at that time the leading politician in the State.

During the years 1902-'03 Mr. Caldwell attended the Divinity School at Yale University, graduating with the degree of B. D. He was then pastor of the First Christian Church at Selma, Ala., for four years, during which time he had such signal success that it was with great reluctance his congregation released him to accept the pastorate of the Christian Church at Wilson, N. C. By special arrangement with the Board of Trustees and the Church Board of the Christian Church he also became Dean of Atlantic Christian College, which position he filled until elected president of the college, in January, 1908.

14

Mr. Caldwell is a man of wonderful tact, of boundless energy, of untiring zeal, of deep sympathy, of fine judgment, of rare executive ability, and the college has gone forward very rapidly under his management. Year by year the faculty has been strengthened, the course of study made more thorough and comprehensive, and the college has more and more demonstrated its claim to a distinctive place in the educational realm of North Carolina.

Under the management of Mr. Caldwell the college has just entered upon a broader plane of usefulness, and it is to be hoped that the bright prospects of to-day may be eclipsed by the full realization of even more than seems apparent to-day.

COLLEGE SONG

From Carolina's broad expanse,
  From mountain, hill and plain,
Where echoes from the ocean waves,
  And rocky cliffs remain.

CHORUS:
  We come with joy and pleasure here,
    'Neath flag of white and blue,
  To gather midst the campus oaks
    In love and friendship true.

While those of Hesper's faithful band
  Shout, "Do and to do well";
"We love the truth and for it stand,"
  Is the Alethian's swell.

For many years may we still hope,
  That A. C. C. will shine,
To lead to light the myriad hosts
  To heaven's sunny clime.

                        G. G. COLE.

FACULTY

THE FACULTY SONG

Our fond recollections of past college days
Viva la memory!
Turn to our teachers and all their queer ways;
Viva la charity!
They taught us aright, tho' they taught us some
    wrong;
We wish to embalm them in this little song,
And as we can't take all, we'll not take long,
So viva la brevity!

To Dr. Caldwell we'll drink with loud cheers;
Viva our J. C. C.!
Grape juice is our toast—no intoxicants here—
Viva sobriety!
He won't let us dance, but he wants us to walk;
He won't let us drive, for Prince might kick or
    balk;
Of college ideals he will evermore talk.
Viva la propriety!

Mrs. Dunlap is mistress of one and of all;
Viva authority!
She doesn't want talking aloud in the hall;
Viva la courtesy!
Uneasy, they say, lies the head with the crown,
But it is we who are uneasy if ever she frowns,
With such a dire fate we'd surely swound;
Viva la rapidity!

Here's to the music that soothes all our fears;
Viva la melody!
It's soft on our souls, but it's hard on our ears;
Viva la harmony!
Here's to art, expression, English, and all;
Here's to athletics, Julian Lane, and baseball;
He'll teach us to win or gracefully fall;
Viva hilarity!

Miss Fanny is standing beside the blackboard;
O, trigonometry!
With all mathematics her head is well stored;
Viva geometry!
She has almost sighed her dear life away
Pounding the the'rems into brains, day by day;
"O, girls, can't you see that the thing that will
    pay
Is reason, not memory."

Miss Grayson came riding down to the South;
　　Viva her A. B.!
"Bennie is the name of my horse," she said;
　　Viva la "Amote"!
She paused in dismounting to pick up a song
Which lodged in the heart of a son of the dawn
Who came in a rush, for love tarries not long;
　　Viva sentimentality!

Mr. Gurganus is most pleasant and gay;
　　Viva la gallantry!
His intentions are kindly in every way;
　　Viva la chivalry!
He's good-looking and has a dramatic pose,
But why will he flirt? Oh, well, nobody knows,
Because his wife lets him do so, I suppose;
　　Viva "comraderie"!

Here's to Mrs. Brown and our breakfast each
　　morn;
　　Viva la hominy!
And our dinners are not to be put to scorn;
　　Viva la "Aleck'ie"!
To everything placed on the table we sing—
To chicken, its drumstick, wishbone and wing,
And when we have ice-cream our hearts loudly
　　sing
　　Viva the dinner Sundee!

We pledge them in a full brimming glass;
　　Viva la faculty!
And we wish we had room for them all as we
　　pass;
　　Viva la company!
Each one did his best to help us do the right,
And make our lives worthy the blue and the
　　white;
We thank them with love,—now they're all out
　　of sight—
　　Viva la A. C. C.!

KATHLEEN L. SALMON, A. B.

Christian College, Columbia, Mo.;
University of Missouri; taught English
Camden Point College, Missouri; Eng-
lish in High School, Raulins, Wyo.;
English in Carlton College, Bonham,
Tex.; Professor of English Atlantic
Christian College, Wilson, N. C., 1906—.

T. R. DUNLAP, A. B.

Eminence College, Eminence, Ky.;
Superintendent of City Schools, Dallas,
Tex.; Teacher at Chickasaw Collegiate
Institute, Audmore, Okla.; Fairmont
College, Sulphur, Ky.; Professor of
Latin, Atlantic Christian College, Wil-
son, N. C., 1909—.

20

ANNA BEATRICE GRAYSON, A. B., 1904.

Washington Christian College, Milligan College, Berlitz School of Languages, Teacher of Languages Milligan College, Milligan, Tenn., 1906-1908; Professor of Modern Languages Atlantic Christian College, Wilson, N. C., 1908—.

MARY A. DAY, B. P.

Syracuse University, Art Students' League, New York .City; Chase Art School, Harvard Summer School, Fry Summer School, pupil Mrs. S. Evannah Price; Porcelain Decoration with Misses Mason, of New York; Teacher of Art Kinsey Seminary; Professor Art Atlantic Christian College, 1904—.

21

FRANCES F. HARPER

Graduate Kinsey Seminary; special work at Knoxville Normal School and University of Virginia, Charlottesville, Va.; Professor of Mathematics Atlantic Christian College, Wilson, N. C., 1904—

MYRTIE 'L. HARPER

Graduate Kinsey Seminary; special work at Knoxville Normal School and University of Virginia, Charlottesville, Va.; Instructor of History Atlantic Christian College, Wilson, N. C., 1907—.

A. E. MUILBERGER, B. M.

Missouri Music Academy, pupil of Harrison Wild, U. S. B. Mathews, Arthur Beresford, Signor Barabuia, Director of Music Century School of Music and Oratory, 1899-1900; Director of Music Adrian College, Adrian, Mich.; Director of Music Atlantic Christian College, Wilson, N. C., 1909—.

ERSIE CAROLINE WALKER

Music Graduate of Atlantic Christian College 1909; Instructor in Music Atlantic Christian College 1910.

META G. UZZLE

St. Mary's College, Raleigh, N. C.;
Atlantic Christian College, Wilson,
N. C.; New England Conservatory of
Music, Boston, Mass.; Instructor of
Music Atlantic Christian College, Wilson, N. C., 1905—.

ELIZABETH ANDERSON, B. E.

Graduate Martha Washington College, Abingdon, Va.; Shaftsbury School of Expression, Baltimore, Md.; Professor of Expression Atlantic Christian College, Wilson, N. C., 1904—.

JOSEPH GURGANUS

Eastman Business College, Pough-keepsie, N. Y.; Instructor of Bookkeeping and Penmanship Atlantic Christian College, Wilson, N. C., 1908—.

MAMIE ROBERSON

Business Graduate of Atlantic Christian College, 1906; Instructor of Shorthand and Typewriting Atlantic Christian College, Wilson, N. C., 1908—.

NELL KEEL

Students'. Art League, New York City, pupil of Mrs. Mary Alley Neal, New York City; Art Graduate of Atlantic Christian College, Wilson, N. C., 1907; Instructor in Art Atlantic Christian College, Wilson, N. C., 1908—.

SENIOR

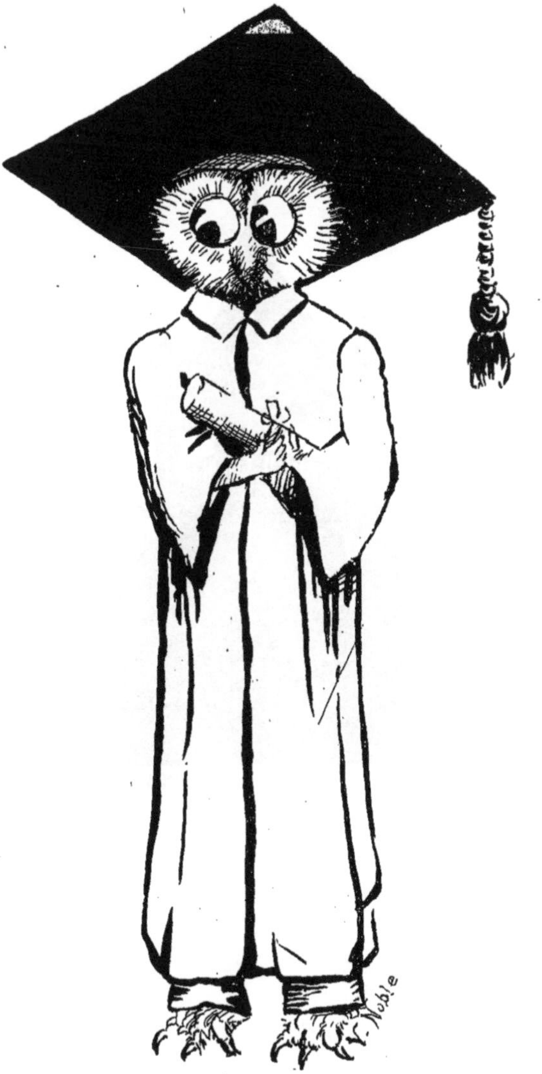

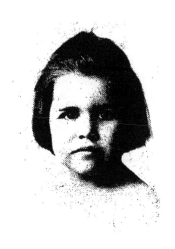

ELIZABETH SETTLE CALDWELL,
SPONSOR SENIOR CLASS.

SENIOR POEM

Our ships glide out on the dark, rough sea,
   From the port where long they have lain,—
We turn from the fort where we trained for the fray,
   To fight on the open and boundless main.

Four years we have tried the compass to learn,
   'Tis now that the test must come,—
Some will no doubt be lost on the rocks,
   While others will safely come home.

Our ships glide out, and we say "good-bye,"
   Our eyes with tears are filled,
But we hope "good-bye" is not "farewell,"
   But to meet again, "God willed."

NOBLE, VERDIE

Art.

KINSTON, N. C.

*"Arm the obdured breast
With stubborn patience as with triple
steel."*

Alethian; President Senior Class; Assistant Editor THE PINE KNOT; Literary Editor *The Radiant;* Secretary Alethian Society; German Club; THE PINE KNOT Artists' Staff.

If determination, will power and spunk will overturn the earth, oh, mother earth beware!

If actions speak louder than words, then our "Noble" girl speaks loud.

Aspiration: To be an Art Teacher.

FARMER, JULIA ESTELLE

Literary.

WILSON, N. C.

"They are never alone that are accompanied with noble thoughts."

Alethian; Vice-President Senior Class; College Editor *The Radiant* (1908); Editor-in-Chief Society Paper (1908); German Club.

The maxim, "All work and no play makes Jack a dull boy," has been disproven in the case of our "Farmer" girl, for she is always at work, and still is a long ways from a dull girl.

Aspiration: To be a District School Teacher.

RILEY, BERTHA LENA

Music.

WILSON, N. C.

*"Like the stained web that whitens in
the sun,
Grows pure by being purely shone upon."*

Alethian; Secretary and Treasurer
Senior Class; Pianist Alethian Society;
German Club; Organist of the Christian
Church.

Music is her soul, her life, her all.
and by it she speaks in a voice divine
and supremely sweet. Quiet and unas-
suming, but dignified, graceful and wise.

Aspiration: To "Cease" going to
school.

FLOWERS, LELA MAY

Art.

VANDEMERE, N. C.

*"Knowledge is proud that he has learned
so much;
Wisdom is humble that he knows no
more."*

Hesperian; Poet Senior Class; Loafers' Club; D. D. Club; Phi Pi Club;
THE PINE KNOT Artist Staff.

If "Flowers" bloom in winter, why
not give them space to live; and living,
why not let them drink in all the joys
of life. No matter the occasion, be it
work or play, the hour is always graced
with "Flowers."

Aspiration: To be an Engineer.

WALLACE, KATHLEEN ELIZABETH

Art.

· JAMESVILLE, N. C.

*"Violets plucked, the sweetest rain
Makes not fresh or grow again."*

Alethian ; Historian Senior Class ; Phi
Pi Club; D. D. Club; Loafers' Club;
THE PINE KNOT Artist Staff.

She keeps up with all the latest fashion plates, and she studies art in order
that she may be more artistic in her
dress. A great admirer, and much admired. Bright, kind-hearted, and a true
friend to those who are her friends,
and all the world is her friend.

Aspiration : Matrimony.

TAYLOR, ROSA BLANCHE

Music.

WILSON, N. C.

*"Music hath charms to soothe the sav-
age breast,
To soften rocks, or bend a knotted oak."*

Alethian.

She cares not for the world, save
what is melodious in the world; she
gives not to the world, save what is
sweet to hear. A lady of few words,
but many thoughts.

Aspiration : To be a Music Teacher.

BARRETT, ANNIE BYNUM

Music.

WILSON, N. C.

"We know a subject ourselves, or we know where we can find information upon it."

Hesperian; Prophet Senior Class.

Thinks twice, but then speaks quickly, and woe be you if you hear not or fail to obey. She is self-confident and determined. Has her own ideas and fails not to speak them. Has her own hopes and ideals, and the obstacles will have to be great if she does not realize them.

Aspiration: To be a Missionary.

WALKER, ERSIE CAROLINE

Post-Graduate Music.

PLANTERSVILLE, ALA.

"One in whom persuasion and belief had refined into faith, and faith become a passionate intuition."

Hesperian; Prophet, Class '09; Graduate in Music, '09; Assistant Music Teacher, '10; Phi Pi Club; German Club; Old Maids' Club.

Aspiration: To "Settle" down.

MORTON, CLEMENT MANLY, A. M.

WILSON, N. C.

"A little philosophy inclineth a man's mind to atheism, but depth of philosophy bringeth men's minds to religion."

Alethian; Demosthenian; Historian, Class '09; twice winner "J. B. Jones Oratorical Medal"; four times Alethian Debater in Inter-Society Contest; two years Editor-in-Chief *The Radiant;* Editor-in-Chief THE PINE KNOT; four years President Alethian Society; two years President Demosthenian Society; two years President Ministerial Association; winner *Radiant* "Poetry Medal" ('09); winner *Radiant* "Essay Medal" ('09) ; German Club.

Aspiration: To study Greek at Yale.

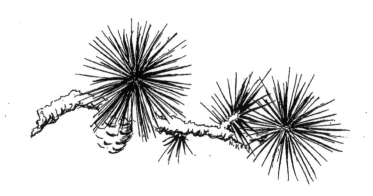

SENIOR HISTORY

ʊ

AND it came to pass—no we brought it to pass by hard, persistent labor— in the eighth year of the history of Atlantic Christian College, and the third year of the presidency of Dr. J. C. Caldwell, that seven weary and careworn maidens, after three long years of study and work, approached the presence of President Caldwell, and, pleading their past records as students, prayed the granting to them of certain writings of parchment bearing upon them the signature of the said president and the mighty seal of the said college. It was an hour of great anxiety—but at last the prayers were answered, and it was made known to all the college that seven young ladies— three in the Art Department, three in the Music Department, and one in the Literary Department—would receive at the next Commencement this important parchment for which they had prayed, provided, of course, that they passed on all their studies and were faithful subjects of the college realm. In the meantime, after it was known that they would receive this important document from the hands of the president of the college, they styled themselves "Seniors."

The history of these favored individuals is very brief, for they have been such faithful learners and such obedient subjects that they have had little time to make history. In September, 1906, three of these important personages entered the realm of collegedom. They were winsome-wee things then. From their babyhood up, they had lived under the shadow of their mother's wing; they had been used to the little pet names of "darling" and "dearie"; they had always had a soft pillow upon which to hide their weeping eyes— but when they changed realms this was all changed. They could no longer "flee to mama with every little sorrow;" they were no longer called by pet names, but were hailed with such names as "freshy," "greeny," "baby girl," and every other name which was different from what they had known "to home." This was a hard year for them indeed, but at last it was over, and back to "ma" they went.

In September, 1907, these three: Flowers, Noble and Taylor, returned, and to join them came four others. One of these, Riley, had spent her "fresh days" at the Baptist Female University, and the other three, Farmer, Barrett and Wallace, by doing extra work in their respective departments were able. to join this near-happy band, for this year the "freshness" had to some extent worn off or at least they thought that they were more important than the faculty or even the president himself, and undertook the very difficult task of running the college to suit their own notion. In this they were successful to a certain extent until one day there came a halt in the ranks and—well their spirits were to some extent broken and they tried no more to run the realm of the mighty president.

September, 1908, found the same seven young ladies back at their work. They had grown more interested in their work and less interested in the things that pertained to the "freshies" and the faculty. They were quite an industrious bunch of workers this year, and so industrious were they that the year passed even before they knew it, and before some of them really wanted to see it close, especially as they had formed a particular fondness for certain other personages around the college realm, which, in common everyday terms, the people called "gentlemen." At the close of the year it was quite heart-rending to see them as they said "good-bye," and—well, it is not necessary to tell the rest, for you all know, and if you do not you will some sweet day.

Is it strange how a band will cling together?

September, 1909, found seven young ladies—for within the three years they had been in the intellectual realm they had really grown to womanhood—and as they walked up the college halls the most conspicuous characteristic seemed to be the self-consciousness of those individuals. And especially after it was granted to them to receive the parchments bearing the signature of the mighty ruler of the realm, together with the seal of the royal court, they seemed more haughty and self-conscious than ever. However, there were certain conditions to be fulfilled in order for them to receive this blessing; and this duty, together with time taken up in thinking of, and talking to, those other beings for which they had by this time formed an undying attachment so occupied their time that they had little time to even be haughty and dignified, only on certain occasions. One great advantage which came to these personages this year, and one which was, to some, the source of more joy and interest than even the fact that they should receive the coveted parchment, together with the seal of the royal realm, was the fact that during this year they were each to be allowed the privilege of sitting alone in the royal parlor with the young man of their choice, provided, of course, that he asked first if he might come. This rule was at first made to exclude all of the residents of the city known as "Wilson," and took in only those from a distance, but as certain of the young ladies could induce no gentlemen from a distance to call upon them they besought the mighty president of the realm to remove this restriction and let them receive callers from the city known as "Wilson." After due consideration this was granted, whereupon one of the ladies who could not even induce a citizen of Wilson to call upon her, besought, with much weeping and lamentation, that all restriction might be removed and that she might be allowed to receive anyone who would come. The heart of the sovereign ruler was touched with pity for this unfortunate young lady, and granted her wish. Since this time all have been supplied with callers.

Very little else of importance has happened, but from the looks of things something will happen with some of these young ladies within a short time after they return home—at least it will if "pa" and "ma" will only give their consent. However, this will be too late to get in this Annual, so we will draw our history to a close, promising to continue it in the year to come, giving in full the revised addresses of the many members of the group.

HISTORIAN.

THE PROPHECY

T O SAY the least, I was very much worried. The truth about it is I
had been chosen Prophet of my class. This self-same class is composed of seven girls including myself. None of us are willing to tell
how old we are; none of us are married; most of us are good-looking; we all
expect to live a good many years yet, and do, at least, a little something towards helping things along. Ours is the class of 1910 of the Atlantic Christian College; no further description is necessary.

Now that I have relieved myself of these few prefatory remarks I will
continue with my story.

Being a prophet I was supposed to lay bare the secrets of the year, and to
foretell the things in the yet unborn to-morrows. This is generally admitted
to be a bit difficult.

It was with this responsibility upon my mind that I strolled one afternoon with a companion out in the country among the pines and into the
sylvan quietude. The magic of the forest and the sleepy, breathing atmos-
phere of the spring day had already touched us with its intoxication, when
we reached a gigantic fallen tree, near a little stream. We sat down to rest
and incidentally to dream and ponder, as near as maids do such things. For
a while neither of us spoke, and during the silence the recollection of my
prophethood came to me and I began to wonder how I should fulfill its duties.

Suddenly, Margaret, my companion, remarked, "It looks as though the
hollow trunk of this grand old tree might be the tenement of some weird
spirit. I have often read," she continued, "in fairy books and the like how
strange creatures, neither human nor divine, inhabited this world of ours,
and some of them dwelt in just such places."

We amused ourselves with this sentiment like a couple of happy children
until we felt a tinge of superstitious awe creep over us.

Suddenly, Margaret picked up a small, dry twig of very odd shape.
Then, standing at the tipmost top of the log, raised her eyes skyward, held
the twig aloft, and in tones of mock solemnity uttered this invocation:
"Spirit of the fallen tree, by the power of this talisman, I conjure you to
appear."

My laugh at her childish antic was arrested in its utterance, for arising from the hollow of the log appeared a fantastic creature, a wizened old man. Tiny of proportion, long white hair flowing down below his waist, and a look of countless years upon him. We sat in paralyzed bewilderment for a moment or two; then Margaret, recovering herself, asked, "Who are you, mister?" A faint smile rippled over his face and he replied, "I am the Spirit of Prophecy." I clutched Margaret with delight for it suddenly dawned upon me that now I could truly read the future of my classmates. In a few words I told the old man of my desire. I slowly mentioned their names to him, while he wore a look half humorous, half solemn, if I may so describe it. As I finished speaking, this old creature disappeared, and I thought he was gone, but presently he reappeared holding a large crystal in his hand.

"Promise to speak of me," he said, "as only a dream you have had, and I will give you a glimpse of things that are to be."

I promised, and he held the crystal close to my eyes. At first I saw nothing but a beautiful opalescent hue, then slowly I was conscious of a change. I was in a vast and beautiful cathedral, magnificent in relics and antiquities of rare old pictures, masterpieces of sculpture, of gold and silver ornaments. The place was filled with innumerable worshippers, all of whom were intently and devoutly listening to the sublime music poured forth from a huge organ in the cathedral. Finally the music ceased, and during the appreciative silence immediately ensuing I looked towards the organ loft to catch a glimpse of this master musician: Nothing seemed strange to me for I felt as though I was one of the multitude by right. And so, when upon a closer look, I saw the æsthetic face of my old classmate, Bertha Riley, I felt no surprise, only joy and pride, for knowing that she possessed musical genius it was only natural that she should attain the highest and best.

Here the vision vanished, and again I was conscious of gazing into the crystal ball held by the skinny old man.

"Look again, daughter," he said to me as I was about to speak, and without a word I obeyed.

As before, all consciousness of present surroundings was lost in the vision I saw. A broad and spacious campus stretched before me, in the center of which, and along the avenues at the sides, were classic old buildings, speaking undoubtedly of learning and study. Scattered about the campus in small clusters were laughing girls clad in caps and gowns. After a little, the mellow clang of a bell in one of the towers issued its summons to work, and all these merry students trooped into their class-rooms. Attempting to follow them I came to a large door and, looking in, saw in gold letters, "President's office." As I looked, the door opened and there seated before a desk sat a stately and gracious-looking woman. Her hair was slightly silvered, and her clear blue eyes, rich with the light of knowledge, rested upon me. My feeling of awe and reverence changed to happy recognition, and crying, "You dear old Julia," I rushed towards her with arms outstretched, when lo! it all passed away, and again the old man and the crystal.

This time as he bade me look I heard him utter a low, dry chuckle.

I was borne along by a great crowd down the street of some big city. There was such a babble of voices that I could scarcely distinguish what was said. We had gone but a short way when the multitude stopped before a tremendous building. For a moment they paused and there arose a deafening shout from a thousand throats, "Give us the ballot"! Then they ascended the steps of the building and passed through its great doors. After much preliminary talking and shouting the assembly was called to order, and a tall, fierce-looking woman clad in sombre black arose from a chair on the platform and advanced to the middle of the stage. "Fellow suffragettes," she screamed, "we down-trodden women who for so many centuries have been the tools and slaves of that creature called *man* have at last arisen in our might and boldly determined to win equal rights with our fore-time masters or to die." Here she made an impressive pause, and the vast auditorium thundered with applause. When silence reigned again she continued, "We have with us to-day a young woman of brilliant intellect, of rare oratorical ability and genius, our leader in this our campaign for the enfranchisement of woman. I have the honor and pleasure of introducing to you Miss Rosa B. Taylor." Here again the house rang with applause, and once again the crystal and the laughing old man disappeared.

This time as I looked into the crystal and glimpsed the years to be I was one of the many visitors to the Paris Salon of Fine Arts. Here the greatest artists of all the world had sent their masterpieces, the creations of brain and brush, to be viewed by an enthusiastic public and to be judged on their merits. There, in the place of honor, preserved for the first prize was a glorious picture, the pride of the artists' world. I looked for the artist's name, and there in modest letters I read "Lela Mae Flowers."

I was scarcely conscious of the old man and his mystic ball before the vision had changed again.

I was in a dear little home, pretty and cozy in its appointments, and delightful to look upon. It was winter-time, the fire was burning brightly in the grate and furnishing the only illumination in the room. In a comfy chair before the fire sat the dearest looking old lady that one might see in a year and a day. She was all alone, and sat—her eyes gazing absently into the glowing coals, her face wearing a dreamy, yet withal, disturbed look. After a moment or two she arose and with slow steps walked to a cabinet and took therefrom several photographs. These she placed on the table beside her, and there taking them in her hands, one by one, looked at each a long time. Now her face was joyous, now sad, and sometimes even worried. I thought I heard her muttering names in accents of endearment. Finally, when the last had been laid aside, and she again looked into the fire, I heard her say: "It has been always thus; I loved each one so well that I could not give him up for the other, and so the old spinster must be a spinster to the end." Before she had ceased speaking I recognized—Kathleen.

My next vision carried me to the year 1920. It seemed I had been reading a great many stories, the most charming and interesting stories I had ever read; not only had I been reading them, but everyone else. The papers and magazines were full of editorials and comments about this new and brilliant author. Her pen name was a simple one—"Verdie." Her real name was Mistress ——. I know for I met her and her husband at a great reception given in her honor. And Mrs. —— was no other than my own little classmate Verdie Noble.

For the last time I was aware of the old man. I was about to speak to him when Margaret called me.

"You have been asleep for over an hour," she said, "and look as though you have seen a ghost."

"I have," I replied with a significant smile.

CLASS WILL

ⵣ

W E, the Senior Class of Atlantic Christian College, realizing that our life is almost ended, and being of sound mind (or rather, as sound as could be expected after four years of mental anxiety caused by "zeros," "demerits" and "curtain lectures" on "How to be lady-like and how to avoid all intercourse with those 'monsters' called 'young men' "), do now make this final disposition of our property:

Item 1.—To the Class of 1911 we give and bequeath our place in college, also our privileges, provided they do not abuse them, causing future classes to suffer as we poor innocent creatures have done. An endowment fund of five cents, given by Miss Julia Farmer, our school-teacher member, who, having made so much money, feels amply able to give something for charity, is also bequeathed to said Class of 1911. The interest on this fund may be spent at the "little store."

Item 2.—We give and bequeath to the "Consolation Society," composed of Misses Grayson and Fannie and Myrtie Harper, all long-faced, sanctimonious expressions, and hope from these saintly looks they will derive much happiness and benefit; also to Miss Grayson we give the half-hour bell, requesting that she ring it exactly on time.

Item 3.—To Mr. Caldwell we bequeath all social periods, especially those "business social periods" which were so alarming to him, and ask that he endeavor to see the latter correctly.

Item 4.—To Miss Salmon we bequeath all "zeros," "demerits," and the "classical edition," "The Young Men I Have Loved in the Past," hoping that it will not produce a melancholy effect.

Item 5.—Remembering our suffering, we bequeath to Miss Day a pair of "rubber heels," so that future French and German classes may have no interruption; also all the stray cats, crippled chickens, ducks, dogs and, in fact, every lame creature from a dog to a lame bug.

Item 6.—To Miss Ersie Walker, our post graduate, we bequeath the settee, which is the nearest thing to a Settle; and to Miss Anderson our best broom, which, if reports are true, will be very useful to her next year.

Item 7.—We give and bequeath to Miss Meta Uzzle all visitors from three-thirty to six in the afternoon, asking that she be extremely entertaining and polite to them; also a repeating alarm-clock, hoping by its aid she will be able to get to breakfast occasionally.

Item 8.—To Mr. Brooks we give and bequeath the "dunce cap" on condition that he strive to outgrow it, and then bestow it upon the next "conceited know-nothing."

Item 9.—Last but not least, we give and bequeath to Mrs. Brown this little book, entitled "How to Utilize All Left-Overs." It contains some excellent recipes for stale bread, liver, beef, and hash, hoping this and the ingenuity of Mrs. Dunlap will enable her to concoct more pleasing dainties.

Item 10.—We hereby appoint Dr. J. C. Caldwell and Mr. Dunlap executors of this our last will and testament, and desire that they look thoroughly into the matter, and carry it out as the will dictates.

SENIOR CLASS OF A. C. C.

FAITH

A paper boat put out to sea—
It bore only Pilot and me—
The wind arose, high rolled the sea;
Then in stepped Fear and spake to me:
"Know you where this frail barque goes?"
I only answered, "Pilot knows."

C.

JUNIOR CLASS.

HISTORY OF JUNIOR CLASS

Verily, verily, I say unto you, many come from the East
and West to march unto the prize—wisdom.

ATLANTIC CHRISTIAN COLLEGE, Wilson, N. C., September, 1907, designates the place and time of the beginning of the march of this determined band. After all had been equipped with the necessities of the march, there came a voice in the form of a command, exclaiming: "Onward! Onward!" the firmness of which made every one fear and tremble. The very sound of the voice transformed the idea of the march in the minds of some from a frivolous to a very serious undertaking. With the banner bearing the inscription, "Attain the Prize," always in the front, the march began under the leadership of captains not wanting in experience, for some are wearing snow-white locks and wrinkled faces, while the locks of others have long ago taken their flight and now have the bare and unproductive spot which is a continual annoyance because of the tickle of the fly's foot. And as our Mashburn says, "We have some who would rather suffer the affliction with old bachelors than to enjoy the pleasures of married life for a season." On we go—some ahead, some a little way behind. We failed to keep very well because we were fresh—beginners—and it seemed almost impossible for our captains to get the same amount of self-confidence instilled into every one in the amount of time, so naturally we at first had to march in an uneven line.

Not very far had we gone before our captains began to hand out liberally the necessities, such as geometry, literature and Virgil, and some of us decided we had not sufficient voices to make renowned singers; some thought the song ugly and old, and in fact dead, while others said, "I will (not) sing of arms and men." Then the band realized that it was marching up a mountain instead of down one, but, nevertheless, a word from the captains, accompanied by a fierce glance, forbade our falling out of line, and although many difficulties and obstacles arose, and the band became very weary, we marched a little ways up the mountain, and at last had reached the first plateau with a solid front. Only a short time was consumed in crossing this little plain, and by September, 1908, we were climbing again. The way grew steeper and steeper, and had it not been for the "sticability" of our

51

captains probably we would have faltered, but all the while ringing in our ears were the voices of the captains, "Near the prize!" "Nearer the prize!" which aroused enthusiasm from the depths of our souls and we marched ahead. A more rapid pace was assumed, and all went well until there arose a spirited contention between a member of the band and one of the captains over "who was who." While the band was standing awe-stricken, a conclusion was reached that the captain was "who," and so our "Pugno" quit the march.

About the middle of the second year's march some were seized with an irrepressible desire to be efficient in the use of the necessities of the march, for now and then they would practice in this manner, *amote, amote*. Although these things drew our attention off for a time, the fact that we were marching was never lost sight of, and we reached the second plateau where those desires which appear invincible were conquered, for "time told the tale."

Now the band was half way to the prize. In this plain a debate arose in the minds of some marching, "Shall I continue or not? Shall I go all the way or be satisfied with having gone only half?" Just ahead was the prize, but still the negative won in the minds of some, and they fell by the wayside; but the majority of our band desired the prize, and so once again—September, 1909—they stepped from the level to the steep mountain side; yea, steeper than ever before. How hard it was to ascend the mountain heights!

Soon after the march from the third plateau had begun, the whole band seemed discouraged because the strength gained upon the plain was almost exhausted, and the last half of the march had only begun, but then was seen in the distance the prize upon the mountain top—and, too, it was known that the halfway mark had been passed and the lesser part of the journey was in front. These, with the thought that that which seems hard and almost impossible can be made light and finally accomplished by patient effort, renewed their strength.

Though we had a pitched battle over Macbeth and Lady Macbeth, union has remained in our ranks, and our band inspired by the example of Hannibal and the songs of Horace have continued the march and have mounted the third plateau and are standing in the very shadow of the prize. We rejoice because, instead of remaining at the foot where our vision was narrowed, we are high up the mountain, beholding the beauties of things heretofore unseen. May September, 1910, find us across the third plateau ready to march to the very top and there know how glorious it is to live, having attained the prize.

HISTORIAN.

JUNIOR POEM

Oh, Junior Class of 1910, come now and let us make our bow
In this great Annual, and then, in 1911, we'll show them how
A senior class should glory make for both itself and college, too,
For surely we'll all records break by knowledge gained and honor true.

And sure am I in coming years our Alma Mater will be proud
Of this our junior class whose praises will be sung so loud
Their echoes will reverberate forever in college halls, I hold,
And thoughts of us will gladly come whene'er is seen "Nile green and gold."

HOPE

I saw the threatening storm-cloud black;
I saw the lightning in its track;
I heard the thunder break and roar;
I heard the wind along the shore;
I saw the rainbow in them all;
I heard sweet music from them fall.

M.

SOPHS

SOPHOMORE CLASS

Miss Grace Lockliear,..........President
Miss Lilly Belle Whitehurst...Vice-Prest.
Miss Susie Gray Woodard.......Secretary
Miss Sallie Bridges..............Class Poet
Mr. Hayes Farish...........Class Historian

Colors:—Orange and Black.   Flower:—Violet.

Motto:—*"Work Up."*

Yell:

"Rattle, Rattle, Bum—

Sophomores, Sophomores,

Here we come."

MEMBERS

Miss Addie Freeman.   Miss Mattie Winfield.
Miss Grace Lockliear.   Miss Lillie Hewett.
Miss Bess Hackney.   Miss Sallie Bridges.
Miss Susie Phillips.   Mr. K. B. Bowen.
Miss Lula Lynch.   Mr. J. S. Rice.
Miss Susie Gray Woodard.   Mr. Hayes Farish.
Miss Lilly Belle Whitehurst. Mr. James Eldridge.

SOPHOMORE CLASS.

CAMPUS VIEWS.

HISTORY OF THE SOPHOMORE CLASS

ʊ

THE Sophomore Class of 1909-'10, after bearing with fortitude all the unpleasant features connected with the Prep. school and Freshman Class, and surviving all threats of the English and other teachers to be "pitched" on exams., assumed, with an air of dignity and considerable self-importance, the grave duties of Sophomores.

After getting acquainted with the duties of such an important class and coming to a realization of their important positions, the Sophomores feel justly proud of their distinctive standing in college life. The Sophomore Class is one of distinction because the college, and especially the Senior Class, always depends upon them to do almost all the substantial work in connection with contests, college annuals, etc., et al., at least this has been true of the Sophomore Class of 1909-'10 of A. C. C. Therefore, with a full realization of their importance, they have these encouraging words to present to the preps and freshies:

Cheer up little Freshie,
Don't you cry,
You'll be a Sophomore
Bye and bye.

In the Sophomore Class are represented North Carolina, South Carolina and Washington, D. C. It is very gratifying, too, to see the spirit of unity and brotherly love that exists between the Eastern Yankee, the South Carolina Rice Birds and the warm-hearted Tar Heels of the Old North State. The spirit manifested among these representatives is a strong proof of the feeling and good will that prevail between North and South. In fact, it has been intimated by some that a great effort is being put forth by a certain two individuals of this important class to demonstrate the spirit of unity prevailing between the once divided sections by forming that union which is inseparable and indissoluble.

One of the most important, and by far the most pleasant, features of the Sophomore Class has been their "Business Meetings." At their "Business

Meetings" anything except business has usually been attended to. The "Business Meeting" has always been called at a time when it would monopolize the last half-hour which the class devotes to the preparation of English, and in every instance the members have been reminded of the fact by one in high authority.

It has been quite interesting to note what an insatiable hungering some of the North Carolina girls have for rice (Rice). It seems that the productions of any other State has been inadequate to allay their hunger. Some have been interested to note the change that came over the countenance of certain of the Tar Heel boys when they awoke to the happy realization that the supply of South Carolina Rice had given out and no more could be obtained.

All in all, the association of the Sophomores has been very pleasant and they feel proud of their record. They urge the would-be successful followers to early say within themselves:

> Can I attain to heights of fame
> Through flowery lanes of ease,
> While others fain the prize would gain
> By struggling with tempestuous seas.

HISTORIAN.

SOPHOMORE POEM

Our Sophomore Class of Nineteen-ten
We hope will be one that will win,
As in the world at last we go
To fight against the mighty foe.

In Nineteen-twelve we'll graduate
And each one leave his old schoolmate,
Perhaps to meet again in life,
Perhaps to lose him in the strife.

But each must go no matter where
The call may fall upon his ear,
Be the pathway straight and filled with ease
Or filled with danger of vast degrees.

'Tis here we practice day by day,
And there we fight within the fray,
And as we practice so we fight,
May each one strive to practice right.

LOVE

The wind was cold, the snow fell fast,
As on the streets folks bustled past
A lonely, weeping girl of five,
So numbed with cold she was scarce alive;
Until at last a woman frail,
Herself but slightly clad, and thin,
Stripped off her shawl and skirt and veil
And made a bed, and laid therein
The trembling child and bore her off
Unto some sheltered nook, and there
Delivered up a prayer so sof':
"Father, save her, hear my prayer."
Next morn the two were found in bed—
The child asleep, the woman dead.

M.

FRESHMEN

1914

FRESHMAN CLASS

COLORS:—Lavender and White.   FLOWER:—Sweet Pea.

MOTTO:—*"Esto quod esse videris."*

OFFICERS

MR. ROBERT ANDERSON..........President

MISS ETHEL JACKSON........Vice-President

MISS MATTIE DUNLAP....Secretary-Treasurer

MISS EARL PROCTOR..................Poet

MR. ARTHUR FARMER............Historian

MEMBERS

Miss Mae Holton.

Miss Marie Bailey.

Miss Anna Belle Kittrell.

Miss Susie Proctor.

Miss Lillian Proctor.

Miss Julia Davis.

Miss Pattie Uzzell.

Miss Sybil Brown.

Mr. Norward Nunn.

Mr. John Hackney.

Miss Cornelia McKeel.

FRESHMAN AND PREPARATORY CLASSES.

FRESHMAN HISTORY

ʊ

D EAR PA:—On arriving here I wish I'd never been born, for you can't know what a Freshie is up against when he lands at college. About a dozen boys met me at the station and collared me. Some pulled one way and some another. I could not see what I had done that I should be mobbed. At this instant the police, as I supposed, came rushing up, yelling, "Stand back, boys." Gee! but I was scared stiff as a preacher's standing collar. Well, Pa, I have often heard you talk about "casting the die" and "crossing the Rubicon" but I think I know what it means since that society mob lighted on me at the station. That night about 12 o'clock a crowd of fellows came to my room and wanted to come in. Of course I let 'em in, 'cause I didn't know anything 'bout the blacking gang. They seized me— tell you what—I kicked, squirmed, fisted and used all the Sunday school words I knew; said I would shoot 'em; said I would tell you and ma both, but sure thing they blacked me just the same.

I thought I was getting on fine 'cause I didn't git blacked but once, and they only pestered me by saying, "There goes little greenie," till the Fresh Class was organized, and I was told to write the class history. Of all the stumps I ever butted this is the hardest one. Pa, I ain't going to do it. Boo-boo-bo, I am going home.

HISTORIAN.

FRESHMAN POEM

I can't write verse—I never could,
And always said I never would;
But now the Freshman Class—oh shook,
I can't write for this Annual Book!—
Has said that I some verse must write,
And that it must be done to-night.

I don't know what to write, or how;
I won't, if it does raise a row.
I'll write instead and tell my Ma—
And Ma, I know, will tell my Pa—
Just how they're treating me up here;
He'll make them stop, for I'm his dear.
                              POET.

PREPS

AT

OFFICERS OF PREPARATORY CLASS

ʊ

PATTIE UZZELL ....President

LENA WILKINSON ....Vice-President

DAVID WINDLEY.......................Secretary and Treasurer

LEO PORTER ....Poet

NEVA HARRISON ....Historian

BERTHA WHITLEY ....Prophet

MEMBERS

Applewhite, Lillie.	Mattox, Luther.
Aycock, Frank.	Porter, Leo.
Barnes, Johnnie.	Scarborough, Vivian.
Bell, Ethel.	Simms, Phillip.
Brooks, R. A.	Skiles, Ed.
Farmer, Frank.	Spencer, Lillian.
Gilbert, Willie.	Thigpen, Herbert.
Gray, Edgar H.	Uzzell, Pattie.
Harrison, Neva.	Whitley, Bertha.
Harris, Edgar.	Wilkinson, Lena.
Hodges, Garland.	Windley, David.
Mann, Triphena.	Winstead, Lamar.
Mattox, Tom.	Woolard, James.

FACULTY DEPARTMENT OF MUSIC

ʊ

JESSE C. CALDWELL, *President.*

ALBERT E. MUILBERGER, *Director.*

MISS META UZZLE, *Assistant.*

MISS ERSIE WALKER, *Assistant.*

MUSIC CLASS.

MUSIC CLASS

ʊ

Bailey, Marie.

Barnes, Johnnie.

Bell, Ethel.

Bishop, Connie.

Bowen, K. B.

Boykin, Hattie.

Bridges, Sallie.

Davis, Mildred.

Dunlap, Mattie.

Flowers, Neva.

Freeman, Addie.

Gardner, Elsie.

Gardner, Ethel.

Gardner, Mena.

Garner, Callie.

Gilbert, Willie.

Gold, Elizabeth.

Gurganus, Joe.

Gurganus, Mrs. Joe.

Hackney, Bessie.

Hackney, Sudie.

Heath, Dessie.

Hodges, Garland.

Holton, May.

Howard, Georgia.

Howell, Lucile.

Jackson, Ethel.

Jinnette, Verdie.

Kittrell, Anna Belle.

Lang, Reide.

Langley, Elsie.

Lynch, Lula.

McKeel, Cornelia.

Moore, Ada.

Neely, Mattie.

Outlaw, Mrs. C. F.

Proctor, Susie.

Proctor, Earle.

Proctor, Lillian.

Riley, Bertha.

Settle, Harriett.

Settle, Horace.

Spencer, Lillian.

Stanton, Mrs. George.

Taylor, Rosa.

Thomas, Ruth.

Uzzell, Pattie.

Walker, Ersie.

Wallace, Kathleen.

Whitson, Mrs. W. S.

Williams, Reta.

Wilkinson, Lena.

Winstead, Daisy.

Woodard, Susie Gray.

Young, Ruby.

THE SCHOOL OF MUSIC

T is the aim of the School of Music to give a broad and thorough musical education, founded on the best methods and latest ideas in use in the best conservatories in this country.

In estimating the possibilities and resources of our college the department of music holds an important position. Music is, in fact, the most popular and the most generally practiced of all the fine arts. It is everywhere recognized as an important educational force and direct means of culture, ennobling human emotions and unfolding the spiritual side of humanity.

It is the aim of the trustees and faculty to promote increased activity and interest in this department.

From the elementary grades to the most advanced work the instruction given is adapted to the individual needs of the student by the best works in the realm of musical literature.

Certificates are given pupils who pass the junior examination, and diplomas are given those who complete the seventh grade in piano music and a two years' course in Harmony and History of Music, with the required literary work.

Albert E. Muilberger, B.M., formerly of St. Louis, Missouri, is director of this department. He is an instructor of exceptional ability and large experience in conservatory work, and by right of training and professional standing is well fitted for the position. Professor Muilberger is an exponent of the Mason System of "Touch and Technic," as also of the Lechitetsky Method of piano playing, and an organist of great skill.

He is ably assisted by Miss Meta Uzzle and Miss Ersie Walker, both musicians of experience and capable teachers. The latter is a graduate from this school.

ART DEPARTMENT

ʊ

THE Art Department of Atlantic Christian College is making rapid progress under the able management of Misses Day and Keel. This has been its most successful year, the class being one of the largest in the annals of the college. The china painting of Misses Day and Keel, the oil painting and charcoal sketching from nature took eleven of the premiums offered at our State Fair. In fact, there is no better work done anywhere in the State, either in china, oils, water-colors or sketching. Our course affords splendid training in each of these branches. The graduating class has some excellent work in oils, done from nature; and the juniors promise, in another year, to excel even this splendid work.

ART STUDENTS AT WORK.

ART CLASS

ʊ

Bailey, Marie.

Eagles, Mrs. J. C.

Flowers, Lela.

Grayson, Beatrice.

Hackney, Martha.

Hackney, Bessie.

Harper, Myrtie.

Hewitt, Lillie.

Holton, May.

Lockliear, Grace.

Morgan, Mrs. Irwin.

Noble, Verdie.

Proctor, Lillian.

Wallace, Kathleen.

Willis, Lila May.

ART DEPARTMENT.

FACTS FROM THE ART DEPARTMENT

W HAT is the most important part of the Art Department? Chickens. The thing receiving the most attention from the art teacher, and in fact the only thing that can arouse enthusiasm, move to tears or recall from that ideal æsthetic world in which the true artist dwells is a *chicken*.

We had been living for months and months in our beautiful dreamland, far, far remote from the realities and common occurrences of the practical world, when suddenly a wee object chipped the shell of an—egg—I guess, though I don't really know. After much arguing and disputing we called the darling little thing a chicken. One by one other little chickens appeared, and for some time it seemed impossible to leave the practical world and the darling little things.

But by struggles and repeated struggles we at last soared to æsthetic realms, and the art seniors, to their great delight, were able to claim the attention of their teacher once more. They really began to feel that their rival, the "darling little chickens," had passed out of existence. But oh dear! how mistaken, for it was soon discovered that a species of minute, wingless birds were inhabiting the bodies of the little darlings just as if they had been planets like the earth. This discovery demoralized the entire Art Department, and for weeks and weeks we worked, with magnifying glass in hand, endeavoring to exterminate the mysterious, wingless species, which we have never been able to name.

Gradually we reached the ideal plane again, and for my part I was very anxious to spend my remaining days here, but fate had not so decreed. Commencement was near, and everything was enthusiastic and inspiring as we wielded our brushes, but instantly a cloud darkened the horizon, and lo! the masterpiece was left unfinished, for a flood threatened to destroy our "idols."

During this descent the Annual staff, with hair on ends and tears flowing in torrents, besieged us. Thus moved by sympathy we spent a week cartooning, silhouetting and illustrating for them. Oh! how harrassing was the worry, hurry, bustle and confusion of that one week amidst the practical, with the Annual haunting us daily, nightly and hourly. Now, wishing it success and pronouncing a curse on chickens, the only things powerful enough to recall us from that supreme sphere, we mount again to æsthetic realms, bidding farewell, forever and forever, to the materialistic world.

V. N.   '10·

Expression

GROUP EXPRESSION PUPILS.

SCENE FROM "THE NEW SYSTEM," PRESENTED BY HESPERIAN LITERARY SOCIETY.

SCENE FROM "IN COLLEGE DAYS."

PHYSICAL CULTURE CLASS.

M.Day.

ALONE ON THE SEA

I'm alone once more on the deep blue sea, with the surging billows around,
I'm alone to sail my good ship free, far out from the horizon of brown.
I'm alone, ah, yes! and my heart beats true as I turn my face to the main,
And steer my ship to'ards the horizon of blue, to never come back again.

A beam from the moon plays over my sail, as the wind bears me farther
    from shore,
And the waves murmur sweetly an innocent tale, as the heavens swing open
    their door.
A perfume of gladness sweeps over my sense, and the joy seems almost like
    pain,
I'm leaving the world with heart-aches so dense, to never come back again.

C. M. M. '09.

THE DEVIL ON THE EDITOR-IN-CHIEF

ʊ

IT IS seldom allowed the devil to speak, especially through the pages of a college annual, for the burden rests so heavily upon the shoulders of those "higher up," and the editor-in-chief loses his temper so often that there is usually enough to keep the devil busy without allowing him to write. However, the devil has beaten the whole staff this time, and while the rest were asleep ran in a carefully prepared essay entitled:

THE DEVIL ON THE EDITOR-IN-CHIEF.

The editor-in-chief is the most important personage on the staff of a college annual—or at least he thinks that he is, and he really gets it in his head at times that he is the whole thing—devil and all. He reasons thus: "I am the editor-in-chief, and since the editor is in the chief I am the chief, for since the editor is in the chief the chief thing about the editor-in-chief must be the chief. Now the greatest of anything is the chief, and since the editor-in-chief is the chief, and I am editor-in-chief, therefore I am the chief."

The editor-in-chief usually tries to take his spite out on the devil no matter what happens to him. If his best girl smiles at another man the devil always finds it out. If he fails on his examinations the devil is of course to blame. If the devil happens in the office some time and finds the editor-in-chief sitting with his hands shoved down into his pockets, his feet stretched about halfway across the room, his collar unbuttoned, his hair standing on end, one eye closed, his mouth about six inches nearer one ear than the other one, and hears a noise like the rolling of thunder, he at once begins to tremble for he knows that something has gone wrong—either that important "business letter," which usually comes each morning delicately perfumed and encased in a blue envelope, has failed to come, or some one has been having a "social period" with the charming literary editor. On occasions like this there are usually two devils on the Annual staff, and the devil that is really the devil is the smallest devil of the two, for the editor-in-chief forgets his dignity and not only acts like the editor-in-chief but tries to do everything himself, acting like the devil as well as all of the other members of the staff.

The editor-in-chief always has a great deal of business with the lady members of the staff, especially certain ones. But strange to say he never has business with more than one at a time. The male members of the staff have very little to do except to stay away from the Board Meetings, and to rack their brains in a vain effort to imagine why the editor-in-chief has so much business with the lady members of the staff.

The editor-in-chief usually does about as he pleases. No rules apply to him. He skips classes, talks to the girls whenever he wants to without asking permission, and marches into the art room at will. There is only one person about the college who has more liberty than the editor-in-chief of an annual, that is the cook. The editor-in-chief is not allowed to visit the kitchen while the cook is allowed to spend almost all of his time in this forbidden sanctuary.

Whenever the devil wants to know anything he goes to the editor-in-chief, and whenever the editor-in-chief wants any work done he usually goes to the devil. The greatest ambition of a college student is to be editor-in-chief of the college Annual, but few want to be the devil. However, it is better to be the devil on an annual staff than to go through college without some distinction. "THE DEVIL."

THE COURSE OF LOVE

One, I love Miss Liza Brown—
Bill Johnson loves her sister;
Two, I went to call on her—
An' 'fore I left I kissed her;
Three, I axted her to be mine,
She said, "Ub course, why yes, sir";
Four, de parson he come round—
Bill Johnson took her sister;
Five, she stole my pocketbook,
And left because I ketched her;
Six, be george, I'm free once more—
I mean to stay so, Mister.

C. M. M.   '09.

ESPERANCE ET DIEU

ט

IT is an old, old story I am about to relate—a story of the early morning of time when the universe was young and when things were not as they are. It is the story of a lass, a lad and a lily—a story of sorrow, of sacrifice and of final success, not, however, in the modern way, but in the way which God saw best for His trusting children.

It came to me in the morning while the dew was still on the meadow, and the roses and lilies awaking from their night of slumbers breathed forth their sweetest perfume upon the gentle zephyrs. It was told me by Rabbi Ben Israel as we stood beside the swift-flowing Jordan, his long white beard waving gently as he leaned on his staff of cedar and told me the beautiful legend which his fathers had told by the fireside from the beginning of time to the present.

Back beyond the days of our knowledge, before sin had entered the heart of God's creatures and when all was not filled with deceit and deception, but when love was true love and devotion, and the lips spoke only the heart's bidding, there lived in the land of the Sunbeams a lass and a lad, her lover. From childhood their lives had been wedded and their hearts beat in unison together. One thought not but of the other, and all day they would sit in the sunbeams and sing songs of their joy and admiration. All the world to the noble Ben Hadad was the heart of the beautiful Rebecca, and the life of the fairest Rebecca was the love of the handsome Ben Hadad.

But one day—'twas in ambrosial summer—came a messenger from King Beltisshazure, calling the noble Ben Hadad to the court of the king of his people. Twenty years had the lovers been lovers, and no day had they spent from each other, and 'twas hard for them now to be parted, but he vowed as he kissed her leaving, "I'll return 'fore the lilies cease blooming."

O'er the desert he sped like the morning till he came to the palace of Beltisshazure and bowed to his king for service.

"I have come, noble king, for your service, and I bow for your orders, my sire."

"Many times have I heard of your knighthood, many times of your love and devotion, and from all my vast realm have I chosen you to do me a service most daring."

"At your service, my king and protector."

"In my palace lies, sick, fairest Mary, the most charming princess of all my vast realm, and no balm in the land of the Sunbeams can give back her strength and her beauty. Only in the land of the Moonbeams can a balm be found that will heal her. Then it can be gotten only by daring, for the princes and the knights guard it closely. Will you go and bring the balm for her healing or give up your own life in the trying? May you choose for to serve those who need you."

For a moment the lips of Ben Hadad were silent as he thought of Rebecca, and of how, should he die in the venture, she would grieve o'er the loss of her lover. Then the idea of duty flashed o'er him—of his duty to those who were o'er him and who now needed help in their suffering.

"I will go," said Ben Hadad with firmness as he rose from the ground and walked forward. "I will go and I'll bring back the lotion that will heal her, the queen of my people, or I'll give as an offering my body."

From the land of the Sunbeams sped Ben Hadad—to the land of the Moonbeams went quickly, and the king sent a prayer to the Father for his safety and return for his service. Many months passed away in the searching. Summer passed and winter came upon him, still he sought for the precious ingredient which could bring back to strength the queen of his people.

In the meantime the beautiful Rebecca watched the lilies as they bloomed and faded. Watched the summer as it passed into winter, and longed for the one who had left her. "I'll return 'fore the lilies cease blooming," she'd repeat as she looked for his coming, but the lilies all went and he came not. Then the winter gave way to the summer and the lilies came again in their beauty, still Hadad came not to Rebecca. All day now she walked 'mong the lilies, and she thought of their coming and going till her form grew as slender as theirs were, and her cheeks as white and inviting. To the world she lost not her beauty, though she changed day by day in her being. Always pleasant and beautiful to those who would meet her, till again came the winter and the passing of the lilies, then she faded and 'twas thought she would perish, but through winter her form grew more slender and more near the slight form she most thought on, till again in the summer came the lilies, then one day as she walked among the lilies Rebecca was changed to a lily, and she stood erect among all the others with her face still turned towards the coming of her lover.

Many battles were fought by Ben Hadad 'fore the balm which he sought could be gotten, but at last after years of endurance he returned bearing up in his strong hands the balm for the healing of his princess. There was joy and glad singing that evening as he came to the palace, but he stopped not to receive praise or presents, for his heart was with Rebecca the fairest. Quick he came to the place he had left her, but he found not the one whom he sought for. Broken-hearted he wandered and sought her in the homes of his friends and his kinfolks, but nowhere he found fairest Rebecca. Summer passed and the lilies passed with it, but one lily stood longer than others and it seemed strangely fair as he watched it, and he thought how much like my Rebecca, still he found not the object of his devotion. Filled with gloom he turned to the needy, and his whole life he gave to their suffering, and his life grew more sweet as he labored. Again summer came with the lilies. In the summer his life was more fragrant, and he ceased to be like those around him, till at last in the midst of the summer he too passed from the realm of the human, and 'tis said that he changed to a perfume and was wedded at last to the lily that had once been his own fair Rebecca. So at last they were wedded in summer, she a lily and he a sweet perfume. So to-day on the banks of the Jordan you may see them at play with their children as they make the waste places more charming and perfume the dull air with their fragrance. Thus true love forever moves onward, and the hearts which are severed in this life meet again in the life beyond our borders.

MR. CHARLIE.

·BLISS

ʊ

Oh for a nap in my big armchair,
   With books and papers all around
And lamp turned up at fullest glare,
   With feet propped up and head hung down.

'Tis sweet to sleep in a feather bed
   When all is well—the usual way,
But the sweetest nap a man e'er had
   Is a big armchair at the close of day.

'Tis when we think we will not sleep,
   But close our eyes only to think,
And Morpheus comes and gives us deep
   A draught from out his cup to drink.

And we drop our book upon the floor,
   Forget the world and life—all this—
Until we pass through Dream's broad door
   Into his realm of fairest bliss.

C. M. M. '09·

LITERARY
SOCIETIES

ALETHIAN LITERARY SOCIETIES

ʊ

C. M. Morton..President
C. B. Mashburn......................................Vice-President
Verdie Noble ....Secretary
C. F. Outlaw..Treasurer
Hayes Farish ....Chaplain
Bertha Riley ....Pianist
Rosa Taylor ....Assistant Pianist
James Eldridge ....Critic
Lula Lynch ....Librarian

BLUE AND GOLD EDITORS

Lawrence Dunlap ....Editor-in-Chief
Mattie Phillips ....Assistant Editor
Kathleen Wallace ....College Editor
Julia Davis ....News Editor
Susie Phillips ....Wit Editor
Mattie Dunlap ....Literary Editor
Luther Mattox ....Business Manager

MEMBERS

Beil, Will.	Hewitt, Lillie.	Parker, Clifton.
Bulwinkle, John E.	Jinnette, Verdie.	Phillips, Mattie.
Crumpler, G. Hinton.	Lane, J. J.	Phillips, Susie.
Davis, Julia.	Lane, Rosser.	Proctor, Susie.
Dunlap, Mattie.	Lang, Reide.	Proctor, Earle.
Dunlap, Lawrence.	Lee, Edgar.	Proctor, Lillian.
Eldridge, James.	Lynch, Lula.	Riley, Bertha.
Farish, Hayes.	Mashburn, C. B.	Ruffin, Harvey.
Farmer, Frank.	Mattox, Luther.	Scarborough, Vivian.
Farmer, A. H.	Mattox, Tom.	Sease, C. I.
Farmer, Julia.	McKeel, Cornelia.	Smith, Claris A.
Fleming, Allie.	Mizzell, Bettie.	Smith, Mary Lee.
Gardner, Elsie.	Morton, C. M.	Taylor, Rosa.
Garner, Callie.	Noble, Verdie.	Wallace, Kathleen.
Gilbert, Willie.	Nunn, Norwood.	Willis, Lila May.
Gray, E. H.	Outlaw, C. F.	Wortham, Annie E.

ALETHIAN LITERARY SOCIETY.

Alethian Representatives Annual Oratorical Contest, February 22, 1910

HAYES FARISH.

C. B. MASHBURN.

Alethian Representatives Annual Inter-Society Debate, May 25, 1910

C. B. MASHBURN.

C. F. OUTLAW.

MY PRAYER

Oh, God, to-day,
Ere on life's sea I would embark,
To Thee I pray—
Not·for the stones from out my path
Thy mighty hand to take away—
Not for less cold or wind or dark—
Only for strength with what I hath,
To battle faithfully to-day,
For strength to overcome.

The way is rough;
'Tis better thus than smooth and straight.
It is enough
To know that Thou art ever near;
And though the storms and billows rage,
And darkness bear upon us great,
Into Thy face, without a fear,
We look, and know we can engage
Thy strength to overcome.

C. M. M., '09·

101

HESPERIAN LITERARY SOCIETY

ʊ

COLORS:—Red and White. FLOWER:—Carnation.

MOTTO:—*"Facta non verba."*

YELL:

Rolly-go, rolly-go, rolly-go-hee!
Hoop-la, Hip-la, who are we?
Rolly-go, rolly-go, rolly-go-hee!
Hesperians, Hesperians of A. C. G. — ―

J. J. WALKER..................President
ADDIE FREEMAN ....Vice-President
K. B. BOWEN;.........Secretary and Treasurer
HARRIET SETTLE ....Pianist
MATTIE NEELY ....Assistant Pianist
HORACE SETTLE ....Chaplain

MEMBERS

Anderson, Robert.
Aycock, F. M.
Bailey, Marie.
Barnes, Johnnie.
Barrett, Annie.
Bell, Ethel.
Boggers, Eunice.
Bowen, K. B.
Bridges, Sallie.
Brooks, R. A.
Davis, Lossie.
Dunaway, J. W.
Farmer, Lucy.
Flowers, Lela.
Flowers, Neva.
Freeman, Addie.
Griffin, Annie.
Glenn, H. L.
Hackney, Bessie.

Hackney, John.
Hackney, Sudie.
Harris, E. T.
Harrison, Neva.
Heath, Dessie.
Hodges, Garland.
Holton, Mae.
Howard, Georgia.
Howell, Lucile.
Jackson, Ethel.
Jeffres, E. M.
Kittrell, Anna Belle.
Langley, Elsie.
Lockliear, Grace.
Moore, Ada.
Neely, Mattie.
Oden, Benj. F.
Overton, Curtis.
Porter, Leo.

Pugh, Lawson.
Quinerly, M. R.
Rice, J. S.
Settle, H. H.
Settle, Harriet.
Simmons, Lois.
Skiles, E. M.
Spencer, Lillian.
Swain, Elizabeth.
Walker, J. J.
Whitehurst, Lilly Belle.
Windley, David.
Wilkinson, Lena.
Winfield, Mattie.
Winfield, Alexander.
Winstead, Lamar.
Woodard, Susie Gray.
Woolard, J. A.

HESPERIAN LITERARY SOCIETY.

Hesperian Representatives Annual Oratorical Contest, February 22, 1910

J. S. RICE.

B. F. ODEN.

Hesperian Representatives Annual Inter-Society Debate, May 25, 1910

J. J. WALKER.

H. H. SETTLE.

DEBATE

DEMOSTHENIAN SOCIETY

Ʊ

Lawrence Dunlap ....President
Lawson Pugh ....Vice-President
James Eldridge ....Secretary
Hayes Farish ....Treasurer
C. M. Morton ....Critic,
H. H. Settle...........................Critic

MEMBERS

Aycock, Frank.	Morton, C. Manly.
Bowen, Kenneth B.	Oden, Ben F.
Dunlap, Lawrence.	Outlaw, C. F.
Eldridge, James.	Overton, Curtis.
Farmer, Frank.	Porter, Leo.
Farmer, A. H.	Pugh, Lawson.
Farish, Hayes.	Quinerly, Millard R.
Glenn, H. L.	Rice, Joe S.
Gray, Edgar H.	Settle, Horace H.
Gurganus, Joe.	Skiles, Ed M.
Harris, Edgar F.	Thigpen, Herbert M.
Hodges, Garland.	Walker, J. J.
Mashburn, C. B.	Windley, David.
Mattox, W. T.	Winfield, Alexander C.
Mattox, Luther A.	Woolard, J. A.

DEMOSTHIENIAN DEBATING SOCIETY.

MINISTERIAL ASSOCIATION

♉

OFFICERS

C. Manly Morton...President

Horace H. Settle ....Vice-President

C. F. Outlaw.....................Corresponding Secretary

Hayes Farish ....Secretary

J. J. Walker...........................Treasurer

J. S. Rice............................Chaplain

MEMBERS

C. Manly Morton.

C. Bowen Mashburn.

Hayes Farish.

J. J. Walker.

Horace H. Settle.

Jesse F. Moore.

C. F. Outlaw.

G. Hinton Crumpler.

Benjamin F. Oden.

J. S. Rice.

Dr. J. C. Caldwell, Honorary Member.

MINISTERIAL ASSOCIATION.

110

ATHLETICS

M.DAY.

Left but gets there just the same.

ATHLETIC ASSOCIATION

ლ

Lawrence Dunlap...............President

K. B. Bowen .... Vice-President

J. W. Dunaway..... Secretary and Treasurer

J. J. Lane .... Manager and Coach

GROUP BALL PLAYERS.

MAIN COLLEGE BUILDING.   BOYS' DORMITORY.

BASEBALL

J. E. BULWINKLE ....Catcher
J. J. LANE ....Pitcher
NORWOOD NUNN ....Pitcher
WILL BEIL ....Pitcher
LAMAR WINSTEAD......................First Base
ALLIE FLEMING...................Second Base
ALBERT BULWINKLE ....Third Base
ROBERT ANDERSON.........................Short Stop
ROSSER LANE....................................Left Field
LAWRENCE DUNLAP.............................Center Field
TOM DAVIS ....Right Field

SUBSTITUTES

Tom Mattox.   Luther Mattox.
John Hackney.

TENNIS CLUB

Ʊ

BESSIE HACKNEY ....President
LELA FLOWERS .... Vice-President
GRACE LOCKLIEAR....Secretary and Treasurer

MEMBERS

Marie Bailey.

Annie Barrett.

Julia Davis.

Mattie Dunlap.

Neva Flowers.

Verdie Jinnette.

Anna Belle Kittrell.

Elsie Langley.

Grace Lockliear.

Lula Lynch.

Lela Flowers.

Bess Hackney.

Neva Harrison.

May Holton.

Lucile Howell.

Lillian Proctor.

Susie Proctor.

Earle Proctor.

Harriet Settle.

Mary Smith.

Kathleen Wallace.

Lena Wilkinson.

Susie Gray Woodard.

GIRLS' TENNIS CLUB.

K.Wallace.

119

PHI PI CLUB

♉

MOTTO:—"Eat, drink and be merry, for to-morrow you may die."
TIME OF MEETING:—After twelve-thirty at night.
PLACE OF MEETING:—In the attic.

SONG:

"If I had a thousand lives to live,
I'd live each one in college;
If I had a thousand minds to own,
I'd fill each one with knowledge,
Then a thousand times each night I'd steal
Up here with chafing-dish and kettle,
For it is no use, while well and strong,
To live in a hospital."

OFFICERS

MATTIE PHILLIPS......................................Past Grand Cook
ERSIE WALKER...................Grand Guardian of Provisions
KATHLEEN WALLACE................Chief Chicken Thief
LELA FLOWERS.................Chief Egg Swiper

MEMBERS

Ersie Walker.
Harriet Settle.
Lela Flowers.

Bess Hackney.
Kathleen Wallace.
Mary Smith.

Mattie Phillips.
Reide Lang.
Neva Flowers.

YELL:

Chicken, chicken, ham and eggs,
Beef and mutton, and turkey legs,
Cream and cake, and custard pie,
Whoop-la, whoop-la, he-ho-hie!

DER DEUTCHE VEREIN

Motto: —

"O Deutchland von all deinen kindren
Liebt keines dich so sehr
Als wir, die fern von dir sind,
Die Deutchen uberm meer!"

Blume:—Die Tulpe.   Farben:—Rot, Schwarz, und Weiss.

Fraulein Bertha Riley ....Prasident
Herr John Hackney........Vice-Prasident
Fraulein Verdie Noble..........Sekietar
Fraulein Mattie Phillips....Schatzmeister

Herr Horace Settle.   Fraulein Rosa Taylor.
Fraulein Callie Garner.   Fraulein Ersie Walker.
Fraulein Lossie Davis.   Fraulein Julia Farmer.
Fraulein Mattie Winfield.   Herr C. Manly Morton.

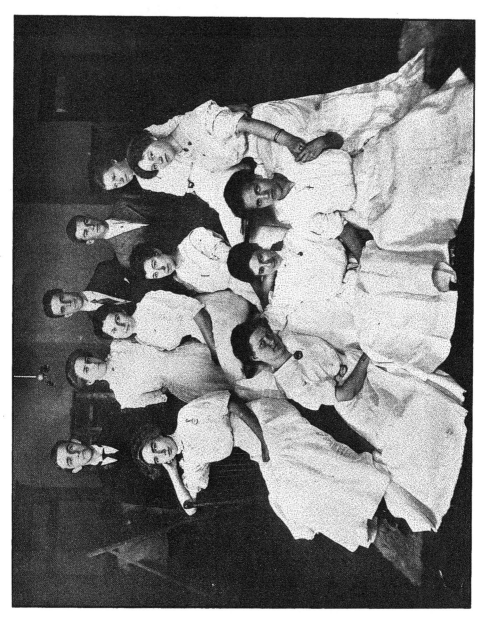

DER DEUTCHE VEREIN.

OLD MAIDS—THRU CHOICE [?]

♉

OFFICERS

CHIEF OLD MAID.............Lossie Davis
ASSISTANT CHIEF..........Grace Lockliear

MEMBERS

MISS PRISSY.....................................Lossie Davis
MISS SISSY....................................Bertha Riley
MISS BOSSY....................................Ersie Walker
MISS PRECISY..................................Grace Lockliear
MISS FLIRTY...................................Georgie Howard

MOTTO:—"If at first you don't succeed, try, try again."
FLOWER:—Bachelor Button.
TIME OF MEETING:—"When the Harvest Moon is Shining."
MEETING PLACE:—Courtin' Alley.

MISS PRISSY—

I'll worry and vex
Until I get "Rex."

MISS SISSY—

My dinner in peace,
If I but had "Sease."

MISS BOSSY—

A fireside—a kettle;
A home—and Settle.

MISS PRECISY—

Any man is nice,
But I want Rice.

MISS FLIRTY—

I tell you a fac'
I've *got* to have "Zac."

124

OLD MAIDS' CLUB.

LAOFERS' CLUB

ღ

MOTTO:

"Do what you must to-day; defer everything you can until to-morrow."

OFFICERS

MARIE BAILEY..............Chief Loafer
NEVA FLOWERS..........Vice-Chief Loafer
MAY HOLTON ....Scribbler
MARY SMITH...............Money-Getter

MEMBERS

Marie Bailey.   Neva Flowers.

May Holton.   Lela Flowers.

Anna Belle Kittrell.   Kathleen Wallace.

Mattie Dunlap.   Mary Smith.

LOAFERS' CLUB.

FURRINERS CLUB

ೞ

MATTIE NEELY..................President

H. H. SETTLE...............Vice-President

HAYES FARISH.......Secretary and Treasurer

MEMBERS

John Bulwinkle,
  South Carolina.

Elizabeth Caldwell,
  Owenton, Ky.

Lawrence Dunlap,
  Oklahoma.

Mattie Dunlap,
  Oklahoma.

Hayes Farish,
  Washington, D. C.

Grace Lockliear,
  South Carolina.

Mattie Neely,
  Plantersville, Ala.

C. I. Sease,
  South Carolina.

H. H. Settle,
  Owenton, Ky.

Harriet Settle,
  Owenton, Ky.

J. J. Walker,
  Plantersville, Ala.

Ersie Walker,
  Plantersville, Ala.

FURRINERS' CLUB.

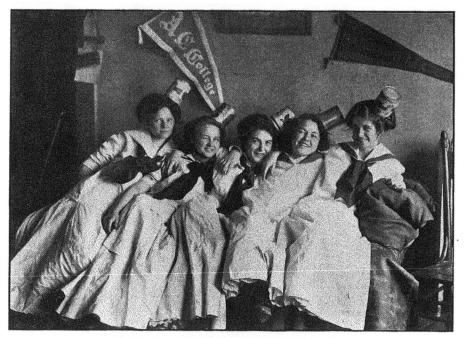

D. D. CLUB.

D. D.'S.

Motto:—"Follow Our Chief."

Ambition:—"To get all coming our way."

Favorite Drink:—"Nectar of the Gods."

OFFICERS

Bess Hackney..................Chief D. D.

Lela Flowers..................Asst. D. D.

Mary Smith......................1st Imp.

Kathleen Wallace ....2d Imp.

Neva Flowers....................3d Imp.

THE "SPOOKS."

The College fool—Leo Porter.

Always "balled up"—J. J. Walker.

"Oh, if I could love as others love."—Morton.

A perfect "old maid"—James Eldridge.

The smartest, brightest girl in the world—Julia Farmer.

The famous art critic—Mary Smith.

"I'm yearning for someone to love me—anyone."—Hayes Farish.

The porcupine—Garland Hodges.

The greenest of the "greenies"—Edgar Gray.

The conceited "greenie"—Edgar Harris.

The millionaire and the intellectual giant—Annie Barrett.

The president of the college—Kenneth Bowen.

The lady principal—Lawrence Dunlap.

The greatest mathematician—even greater than Pythagoras or Euclid—Sease.

"Great guns! I'll be an old maid in spite of all my efforts."—Verdie Noble.

The most stupid boy—Horace Settle.

Two love-sick 'kids"—Harriet Settle and Tom Uzzell.

A girl old enough to correspond with young men, but entirely too young to converse with them—Mattie Dunlap.

"Oh, don't stand before me; I want my pretty eyes to show."—Reide Lang.

"When will these three meet again": Garland Hodges, soap and water?

"Oh, I wish Mr. Farish would not be so sentimental. Because we have the sentimental part in the play, he thinks he must keep up his silly love-making after we leave the stage."—Lossie Davis.

HOW TO GET OUT A GOOD ANNUAL

FIRST, let a young man and a young lady who, apparently, have a fondness for each other's society; in some way designate themselves as editor-in-chief and assistant, respectively, of the proposed Annual. Then they must, by all means, contrive to have no seniors on the editorial staff, except those who are blind as moles, lest the keen-sighted senior should observe cupid stealthily spying around. The disposal of the seniors may be accomplished either by straightforward or fraudulent means, since it is so very essential; "honesty is (no longer) the best policy."

The seniors out of the way, the editor-in-chief and assistant must have a meeting for the purpose of selecting editors. During this meeting they may enumerate the classes from "prep." to senior, discussing each individual in the different classes—their chief characteristics, merits and demerits. Perhaps you will think this a poor plan for selecting editors, and one taking entirely too much time, but, my good friend, it is particularly essential for the editor-in-chief to spend all the time possible with the assistant, planning and talking everything under the sun except the Annual.

The necessary editors having been chosen on account of their blindness and stupidity, we are ready for business. Now the entire college must be thrown into confusion and work almost suspended for a week, while the cuts are made. During this week of tumultuous confusion the club organizations should be increased at least 100 per cent in order to give more cuts for the Annual and to make the reign of confusion longer. The following week, assail the college artists for silhouettes, cartoons, etc., giving them only a week to do the work.

Now comes the literary work. Well, that is a small matter, just call on the seniors who are so learned and intimate with the classics as to tell you that Shakespeare is an American, and that Jeffrey Chaucer is a descendant of Pocahontas, and also that Whittier is the greatest poet that England has ever produced.

The material all ready, the editor-in-chief and the assistant have a delightful treat in store, since to arrange it the aid of the other editors is, of course, unnecessary.

By the way, I had almost forgotten to say it is perfect nonsense to begin an Annual—as is usually the case—six or eight months before the publication is to appear. Two months is all the time necessary—a month and a half for the editors to plan and arrange, and two weeks for the publishers to get it out. If, in that time, the editor-in-chief and the assistant are unable "to line up their ducks" it is a hopeless case and had better be abandoned.

V. N. '10·

E PLURIBUS UNUM

ぴ

I.

A maiden fair, with boughten hair
　　And teeth sent to her from the store,
Reclined within her big armchair,
　　As she had oft reclined before.

And looking through the mirror-glass,
　　The powder-puff plied free and fas'ᵗ
Upon her rosy cheek, ye saint,
　　Already she had 'plied the paint.

And thought, "How fair I'll be to-night;
　　And surely Jack will halt no more
Between me and that awful fright—
　　That ugly, homely, Mary Moore."

II.

Jack came within an hour's time,—
　　She blushed, but it could hardly shine,
For powder hid the natural look—
　　Her manners were just like the book.

Of course he had to stay a·while
　　And chat and laugh and talk and
　　　　smile,
And tell her how he loved her, too,—
　　You know that's how men have to do.

But all the time he was thinking o'er
　　The simple grace of Mary Moore.
Not quite so near a fashion plate,
　　But near the beauty God first sate.

III.

The years rolled by, more hair was
　　　　bought,
　　More teeth, and paint, and powder
　　　　sought,
But for a woman old in years,
　　A maiden lady filled with tears.

While Jack and Mary lived in bliss,
　　And Mary often thought on this:
"How did I win this noble man?
　　'Tis hard for me to understan'."

But Jack within his heart knew why,
　　And did not tell, but let it lie
'Til little Mary grew to age
　　And then he told her—father, sage.

MORAL:

The beauty made by human han'
　　May sway the tongue of flatt'ring
　　　　man,
But the simple beauty Nature gave
　　'Lone can the heart of man enslave.

　　　　　　　　　　　　CLEM.

MY VERSE

They say that I must write some verse
No matter—good or bad, or worse,
Just so I write and write it quick—
(The deuce, this ink won't flow—it's thick.)

There was a girl named Molly,
    So gay and free and jolly;
She went to the gym. and tried to swim
    On an acting bar, by golly.

She weighed around two-thirty;
    A boy—it was quite dirty—
Had broke the bar and hid the scar,
    She took a dive—it "hurte."

A naughty lad stole from his dad
    A plug of Schnapps tobacker
And ran away—I heard him say—
    That he might chew and whacker.

He took a chew, then one or two,
    And then—'tis sad to show it—
His breakfast disagreed with him;
    The rest, of course, you know it.

                                        CLEM.

THE EVOLUTION OF LOVE

Love, to the girl of sweet sixteen
  Is the boy that's sweet and cute;
No matter his name, that's out of the game;
  No matter his worth, he'll suit.

Love, to the girl of eighteen years
  Is the lad with taffy to let;
He must bring her gum, and flatter her some,
  And he is all right, you bet.

Love, to the girl of twenty-one
  Is the man who has the cash;
His face may be rough, if he has the stuff
  He's sure to make a mash.

Love, to the girl of twenty-four
  Is a man that's a man indeed;
No "cutie" will go, no flatterer or crow,
  But a man with a mind and creed.

Love, to the girl of thirty, ah!
  Not quite so choice to-day;
A boy, a man, or—you understand—
  Anyone who comes her way.

Love, to the maid of forty—oh!
  Dear Lord, anyone will do;
Something with pants, or a monkey that'll dance;
  Dear Lord, just send her two.

A Conceited Man.

Publications

RADIANT STAFF

ᛌ

H. H. SETTLE .... Editor-in-Chief

C. M. MORTON .... Assistant Editor

K. B. BOWEN .... Business Manager

HAYES FARISH .... Assistant Business Manager

LOSSIE DAVIS ⎫
REIDE LANG   ⎬ .... Literary Editors
VERDIE NOBLE ⎭

C. B. MASHBURN ⎫
MATTIE NEELY   ⎬ .... Wit Editors

MATTIE PHILLIPS .... Ex Collegio

J. J. WALKER   ⎫
LAWRENCE DUNLAP ⎬ .... College Editors

LAWSON PUGH .... Exchange Editor

J. GURGANUS .... Athletic Editor

"RADIANT" STAFF.

THE PINE KNOT STAFF

C. MANLY MORTON..................................Editor-in-Chief

MISS VERDIE NOBLE ....Assistant Editor

MISS ERSIE WALKER ....Departmental Editor

JAMES JOSEPH WALKER............................Society Editor

MISS BERTHA RILEY ....Senior Editor

MISS LOSSIE DAVIS ....Junior Editor

MISS BESSIE HACKNEY...........................Sophomore Editor

MISS JULIA DAVIS...............................Freshman Editor

HAYES FARISH..................................Business Manager

LAWRENCE DUNLAP.....................Assistant Business Manager

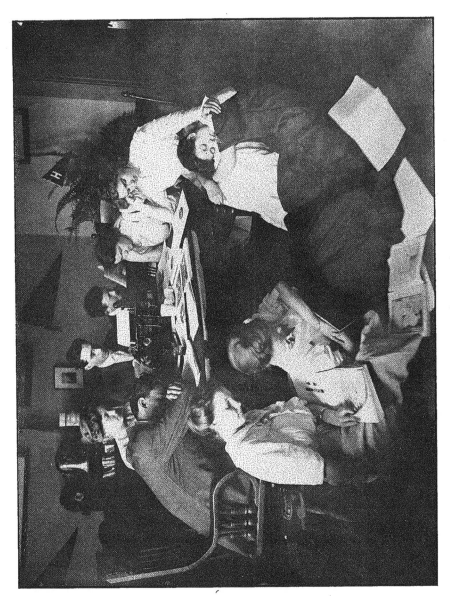

"THE PINE KNOT" STAFF.—'TIS DONE.

Hard at work on caytoons.

OUR ARTISTS

Miss Mary A. Day.

Miss Nell Keel.

Miss Verdie Noble.

Miss Lela Flowers.

Miss Mary Smith.

Miss Kathleen Wallace.

EDITORIAL

ʊ

VOLUME I. of THE PINE KNOT is, in your hands. You have probably looked at its illustrations and read its messages; you have seen more of the real "college life" at Atlantic Christian College than ever before; you have had brought to your mind the pleasant remembrances of your own college days.; you have looked eagerly for the face of someone you know; you have noted the growth and development of the college; you have laughed at the humor, and admired the articles of a serious nature. Now, as you close the book, you have upon your lips either words of criticism or of consideration—probably both. We know you have found many mistakes, and many points which could be strengthened, but we hope at the same time you have found many things to admire and to interest you. This being the first Annual issued by the students of Atlantic Christian College, the work has, of course, been confronted by many difficulties and disadvantages; but we have done our best, and hope that you will temper your criticism with mercy, and unite with the editors in the future to overcome all the shortcomings of this issue.

We appreciate every kind word which has been spoken concerning us and our work; we appreciate every smile, and every kind feeling; we appreciate your support, and your co-operation; we have done our best; we have labored early and late; we have borne more, probably, than you know, but we have borne it all freely and willingly, and all that we ask in return is your kind wishes, and your promise to ever keep THE PINE KNOT alive, and to strive to make each succeeding issue better than the last, until it shall take its stand in the very forefront of the college annuals of the world, and then not be content until it shall set a quicker pace for all the others to follow.

With these words, and with our work to speak for itself, and again thanking you and asking your interest and support for the future, we make our final bow, and bid you "good-bye." THE EDITORS.

Interior of PRIVETT & CO.'S Jewelry Store, Wilson, N. C.
MANUFACTURING JEWELERS
202 EAST NASH STREET   TELEPHONE 141

The
ALPHA PHOTO
ENGRAVING
COMPANY
INCORPORATED
Artists & Engravers
N.E. COR. HOWARD AND FAYETTE STS.
BALTIMORE, MD.

Florist

"EASY TO REMEMBER"

Wedding Bouquets Arranged in Artistic Style.
Floral Offerings Beautifully Designed at Short Notice.
Mail, Telegraph and Telephone Orders Promptly Executed.

DECORATIVE FLOWERING
and Vegetable Plants in Season

Schwartz, Kirwin & Fauss

"If we made it for Gold, it's Gold."

RELIABLE MANUFACTURERS

OF

Class, College and Fraternity Pins

MEDALS

PRIZES FOR GAMES, ETC.

♉ ♉

42 Barclay Street   *NEW YORK*

152

Lightning Source UK Ltd.
Milton Keynes UK
UKHW022313211118
332685UK00005B/389/P